GRAPHIC SCIENCE

THE BASICS OF

CELL LIFE

WITH MAX AXIOM SUPER SCIENTIST

by Amber J. Keyser, PhD

illustrated by Cynthia Martin and Barbara Schulz

Consultant:

Monte Westerfield, PhD

Professor of Biology

University of Oregon, Eugene

Capstone
press

Mankato, Minnesota

Graphic Library is published by Capstone Press,
1710 Roe Crest Drive, North Mankato, Minnesota 56003.
www.capstonepub.com

Printed in the United States of America in Stevens Point, Wisconsin.
022013
007180R

Books published by Capstone Press are manufactured with paper containing at least 10 percent post-consumer waste.

Library of Congress Cataloging-in-Publication Data
Keyser, Amber J., PhD
The basics of cell life with Max Axiom, super scientist / by Amber J. Keyser, PhD; illustrated by Cynthia Martin and Barbara Schulz.
p. cm. — (Graphic library. Graphic science)
Summary: "In graphic novel format, follows the adventures of Max Axiom as he explains the science behind plant and animal cells" — Provided by publisher.
Includes bibliographical references and index.
ISBN 978-1-4296-3414-4 (library binding)
ISBN 978-1-4296-3904-0 (softcover)
1. Cells — Juvenile literature. I. Martin, Cynthia, 1961– ill. II. Schulz, Barbara (Barbara Jo) III. Title. IV. Series.
QH582.5.K49 2010
571.6 — dc22 2009003952

Designer
Alison Thiele

Cover Artist
Tod G. Smith

Cover Colorist
Krista Ward

Colorist
Matt Webb

Editor
Lori Shores

TABLE of CONTENTS

BUILDING BLOCKS OF LIFE

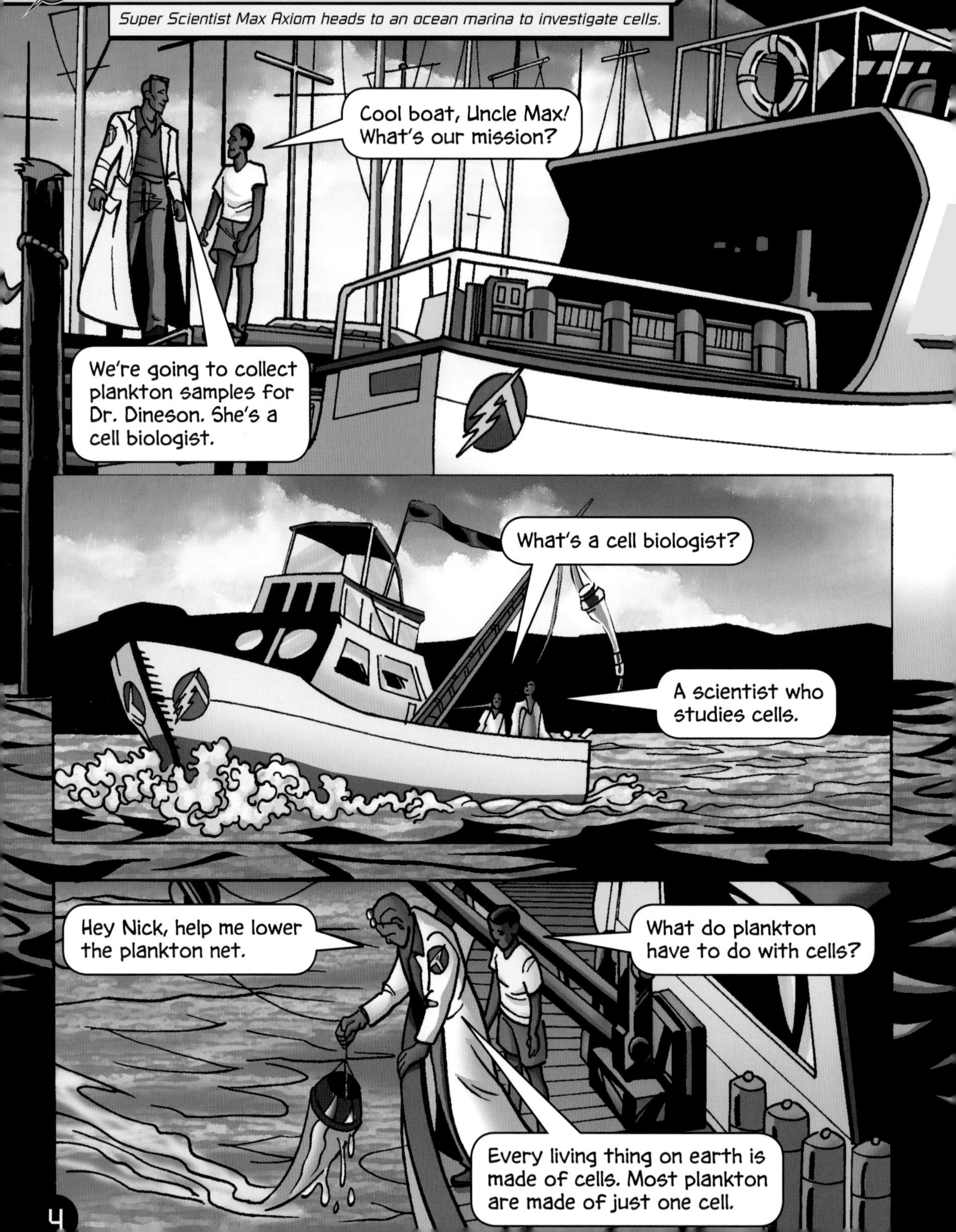
Super Scientist Max Axiom heads to an ocean marina to investigate cells.
Cool boat, Uncle Max! What's our mission?
We're going to collect plankton samples for Dr. Dineson. She's a cell biologist.
What's a cell biologist?
A scientist who studies cells.
Hey Nick, help me lower the plankton net.
What do plankton have to do with cells?
Every living thing on earth is made of cells. Most plankton are made of just one cell.

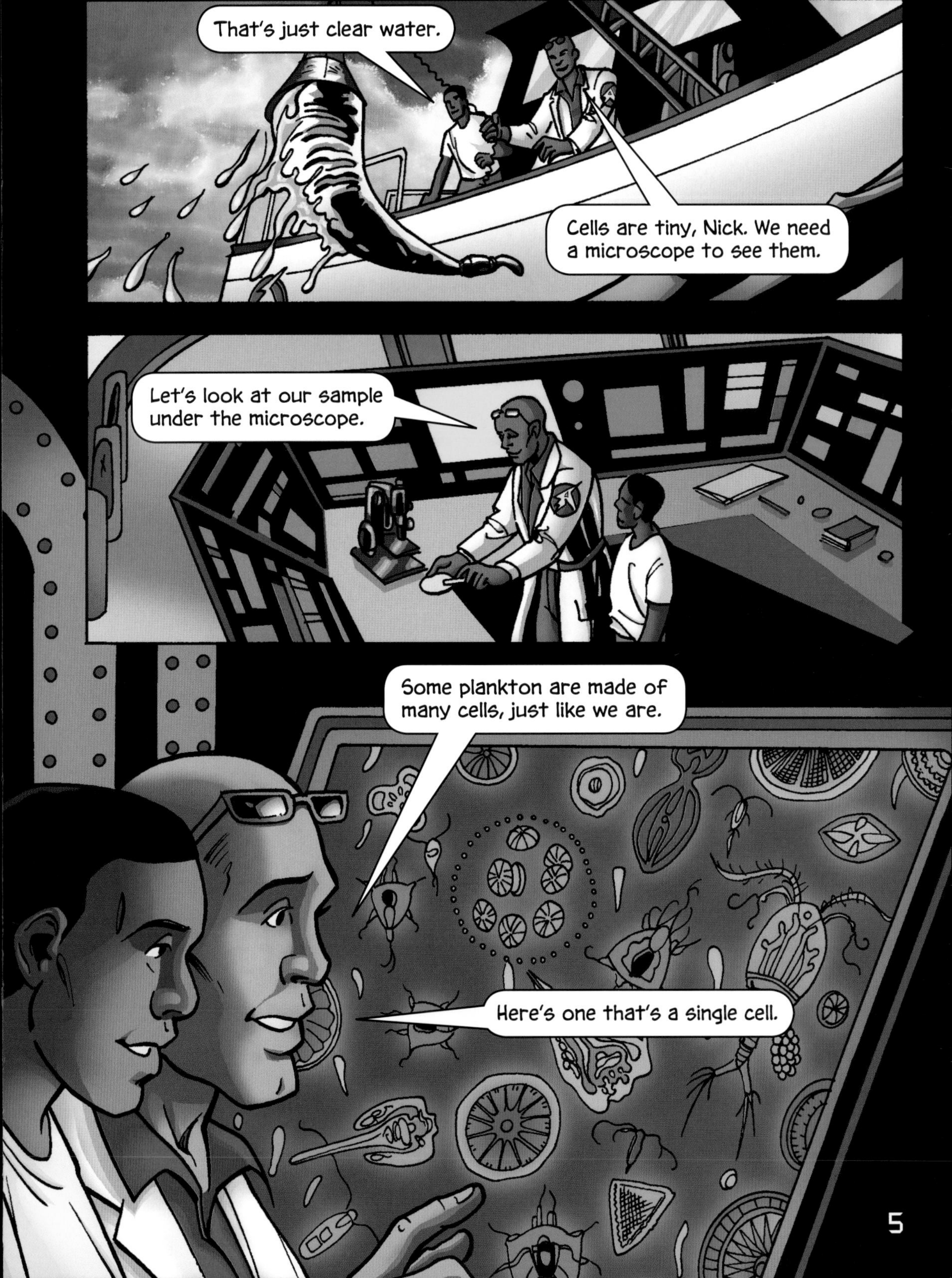
That's just clear water.
Cells are tiny, Nick. We need a microscope to see them.
Let's look at our sample under the microscope.
Some plankton are made of many cells, just like we are.
Here's one that's a single cell.

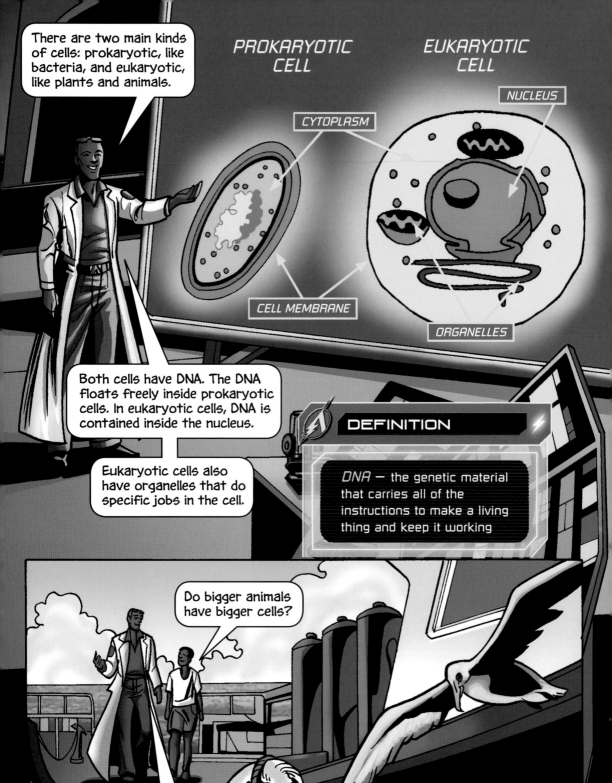

There are two main kinds of cells: prokaryotic, like bacteria, and eukaryotic, like plants and animals.

PROKARYOTIC CELL

EUKARYOTIC CELL

NUCLEUS

CYTOPLASM

CELL MEMBRANE

ORGANELLES

Both cells have DNA. The DNA floats freely inside prokaryotic cells. In eukaryotic cells, DNA is contained inside the nucleus.

Eukaryotic cells also have organelles that do specific jobs in the cell.

DEFINITION

DNA — the genetic material that carries all of the instructions to make a living thing and keep it working

Do bigger animals have bigger cells?

Nope, just a lot more of them. The human body is made up of 50 to 60 trillion cells!

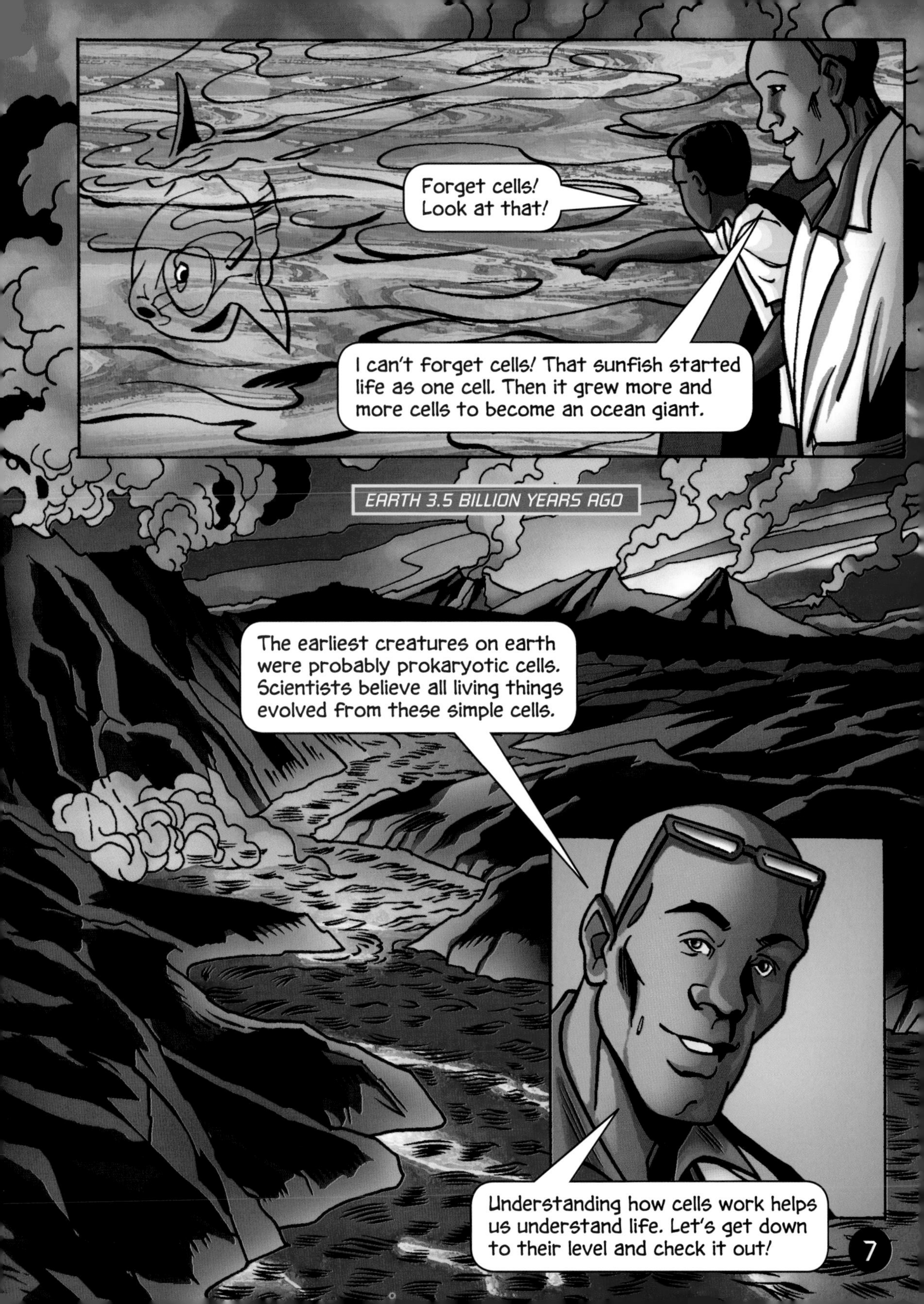
Forget cells! Look at that!
I can't forget cells! That sunfish started life as one cell. Then it grew more and more cells to become an ocean giant.
EARTH 3.5 BILLION YEARS AGO
The earliest creatures on earth were probably prokaryotic cells. Scientists believe all living things evolved from these simple cells.
Understanding how cells work helps us understand life. Let's get down to their level and check it out!

SECTION 2 | CELL METABOLISM

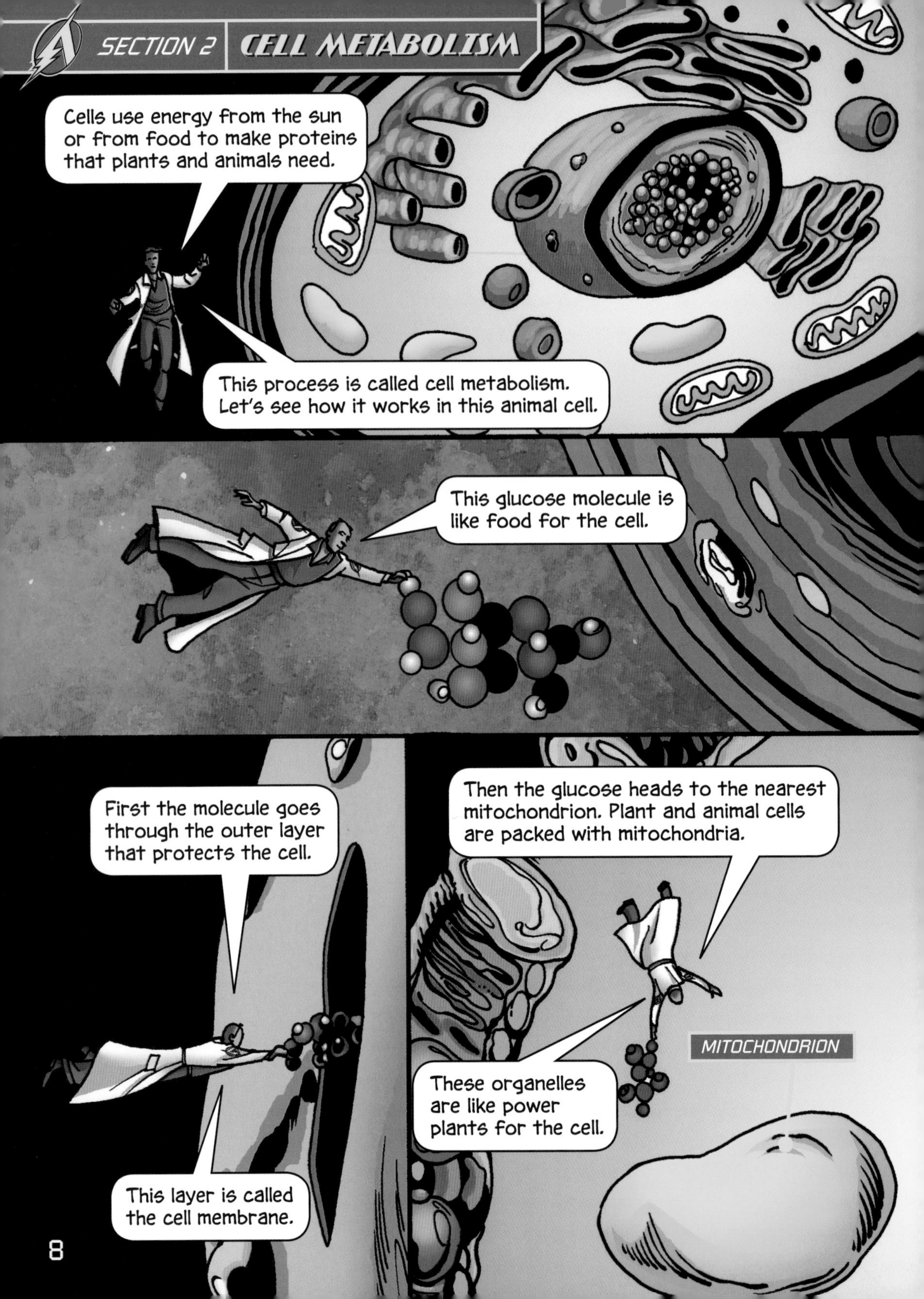
Cells use energy from the sun or from food to make proteins that plants and animals need.
This process is called cell metabolism. Let's see how it works in this animal cell.
This glucose molecule is like food for the cell.
First the molecule goes through the outer layer that protects the cell.
This layer is called the cell membrane.
Then the glucose heads to the nearest mitochondrion. Plant and animal cells are packed with mitochondria.
MITOCHONDRION
These organelles are like power plants for the cell.

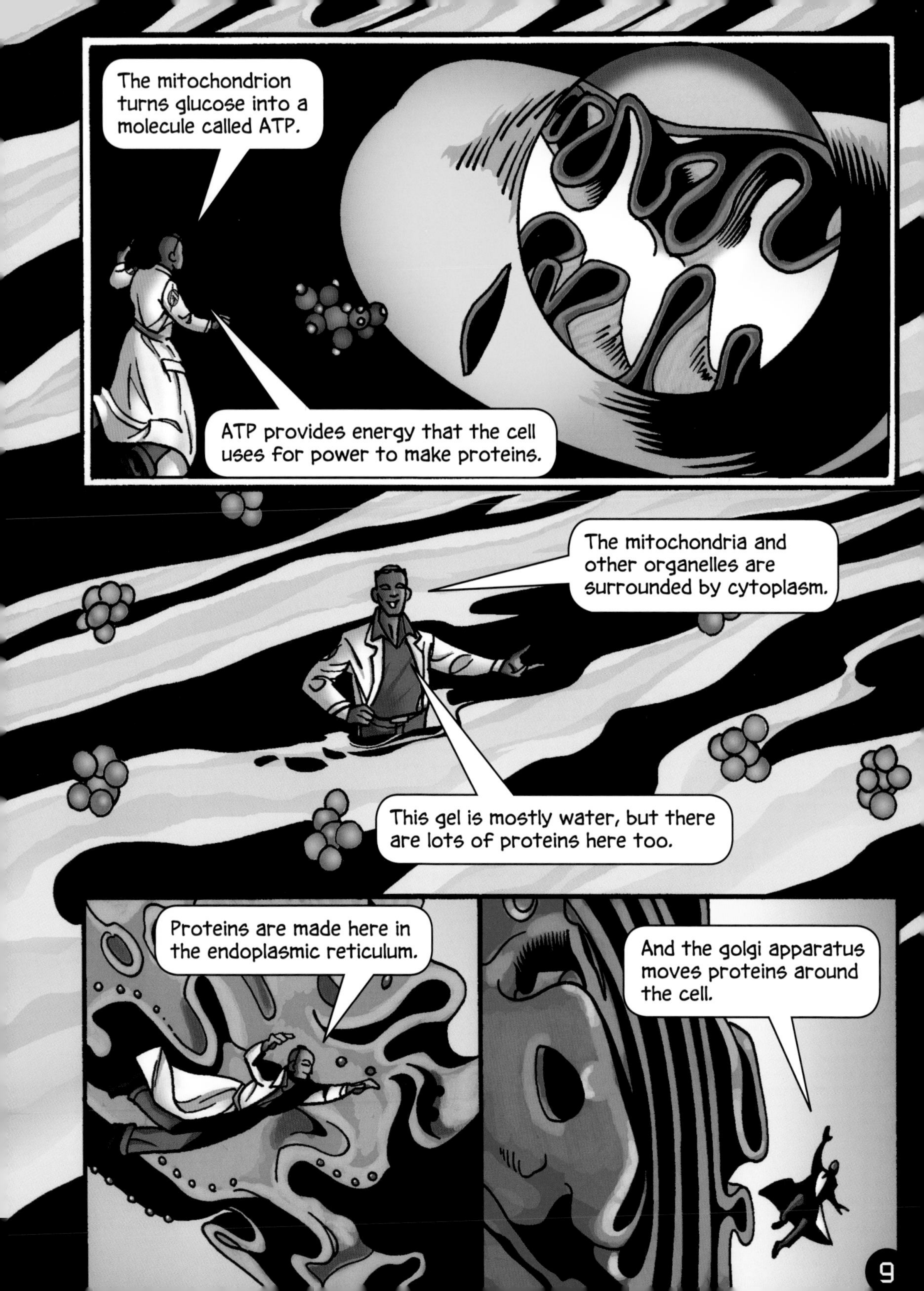
The mitochondrion turns glucose into a molecule called ATP.
ATP provides energy that the cell uses for power to make proteins.
The mitochondria and other organelles are surrounded by cytoplasm.
This gel is mostly water, but there are lots of proteins here too.
Proteins are made here in the endoplasmic reticulum.
And the golgi apparatus moves proteins around the cell.

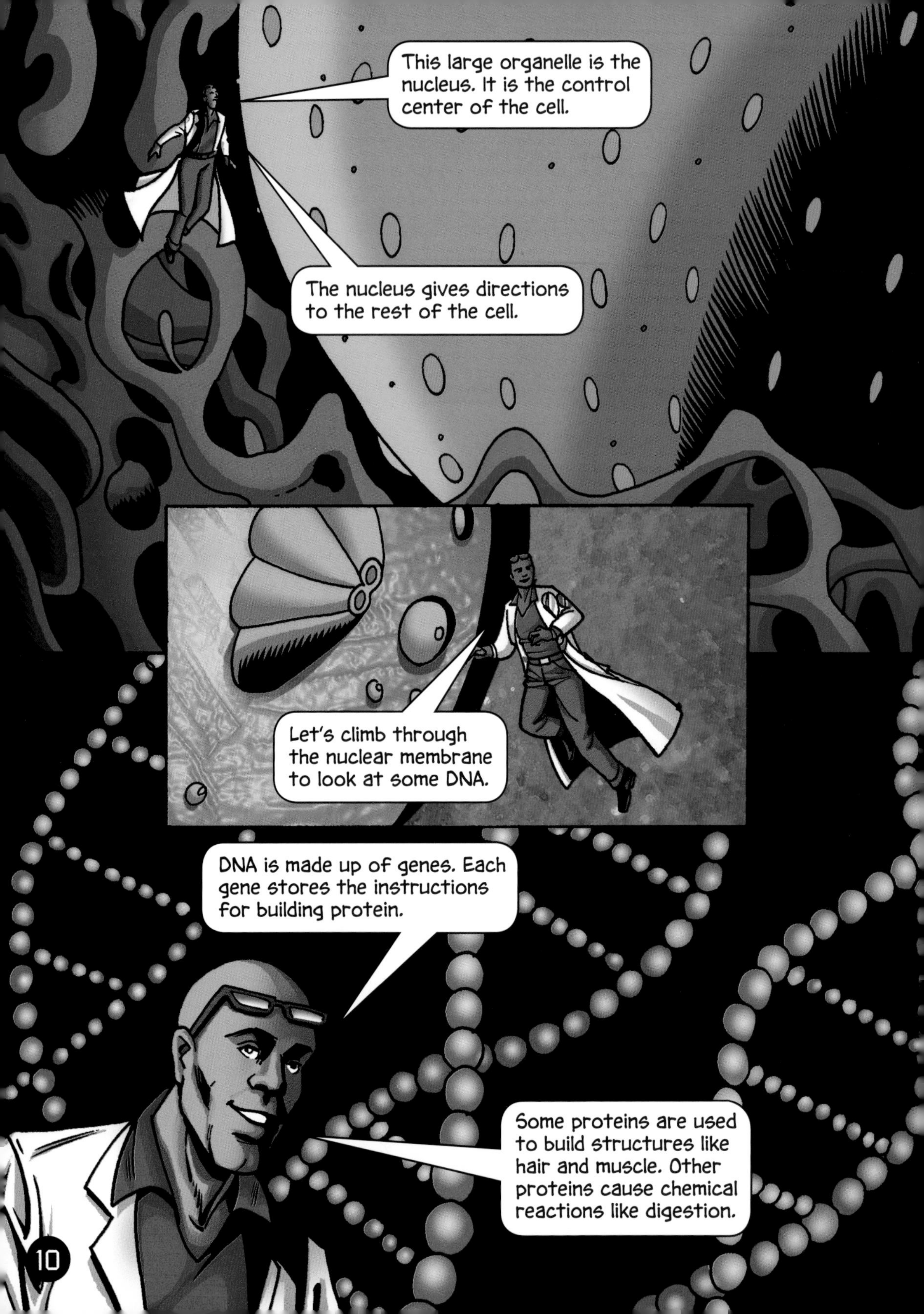
This large organelle is the nucleus. It is the control center of the cell.
The nucleus gives directions to the rest of the cell.
Let's climb through the nuclear membrane to look at some DNA.
DNA is made up of genes. Each gene stores the instructions for building protein.
Some proteins are used to build structures like hair and muscle. Other proteins cause chemical reactions like digestion.

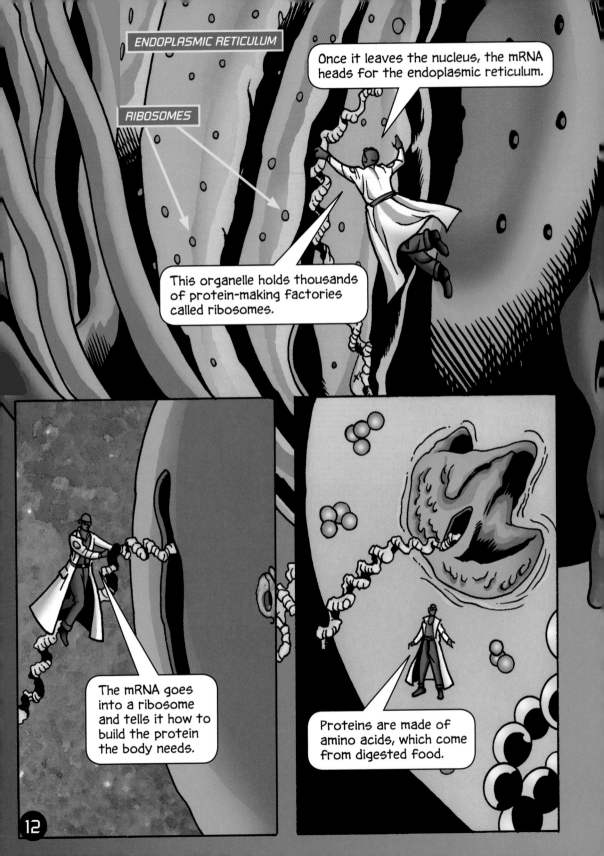

ENDOPLASMIC RETICULUM

RIBOSOMES

Once it leaves the nucleus, the mRNA heads for the endoplasmic reticulum.

This organelle holds thousands of protein-making factories called ribosomes.

The mRNA goes into a ribosome and tells it how to build the protein the body needs.

Proteins are made of amino acids, which come from digested food.

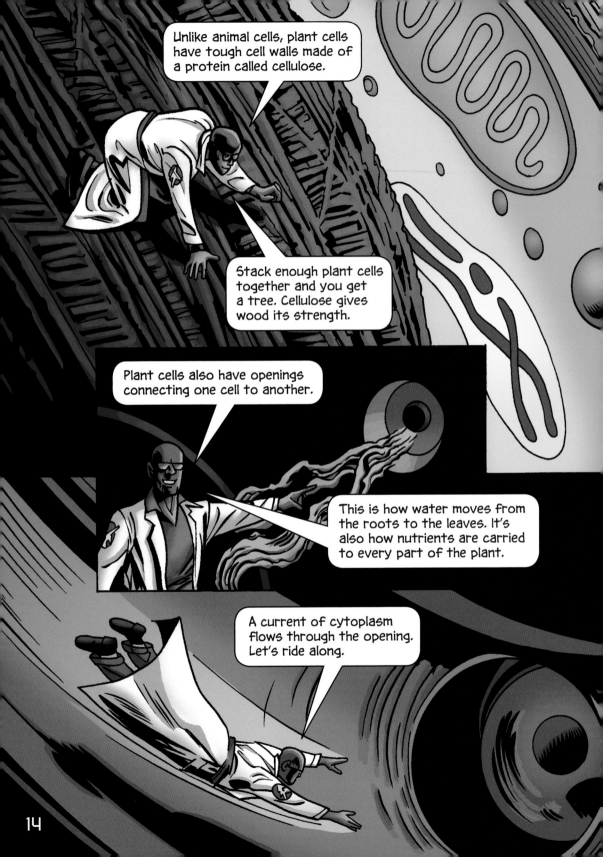

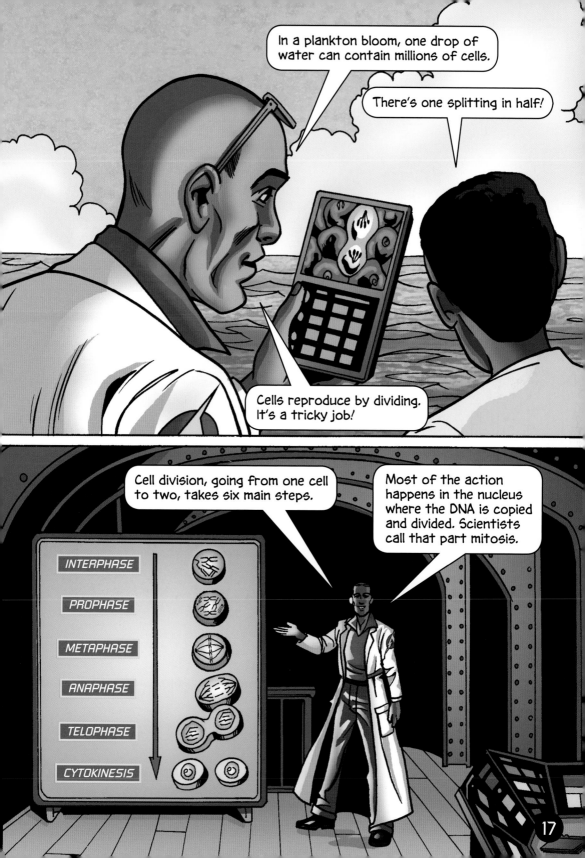

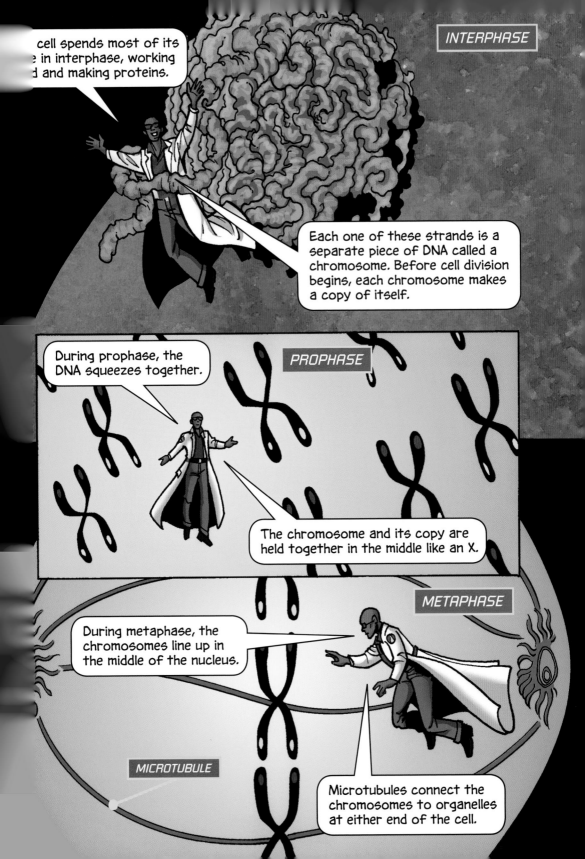

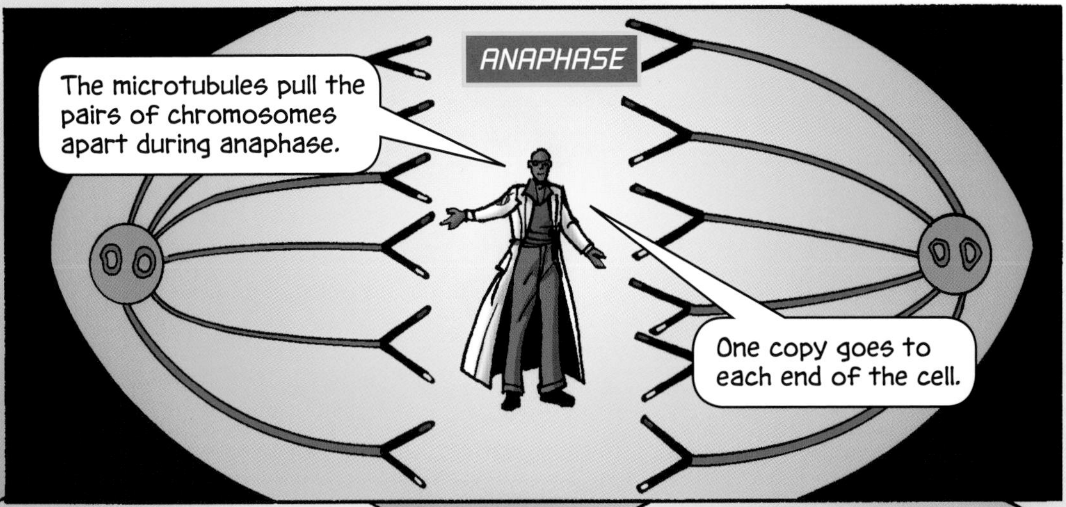
ANAPHASE
The microtubules pull the pairs of chromosomes apart during anaphase.
One copy goes to each end of the cell.

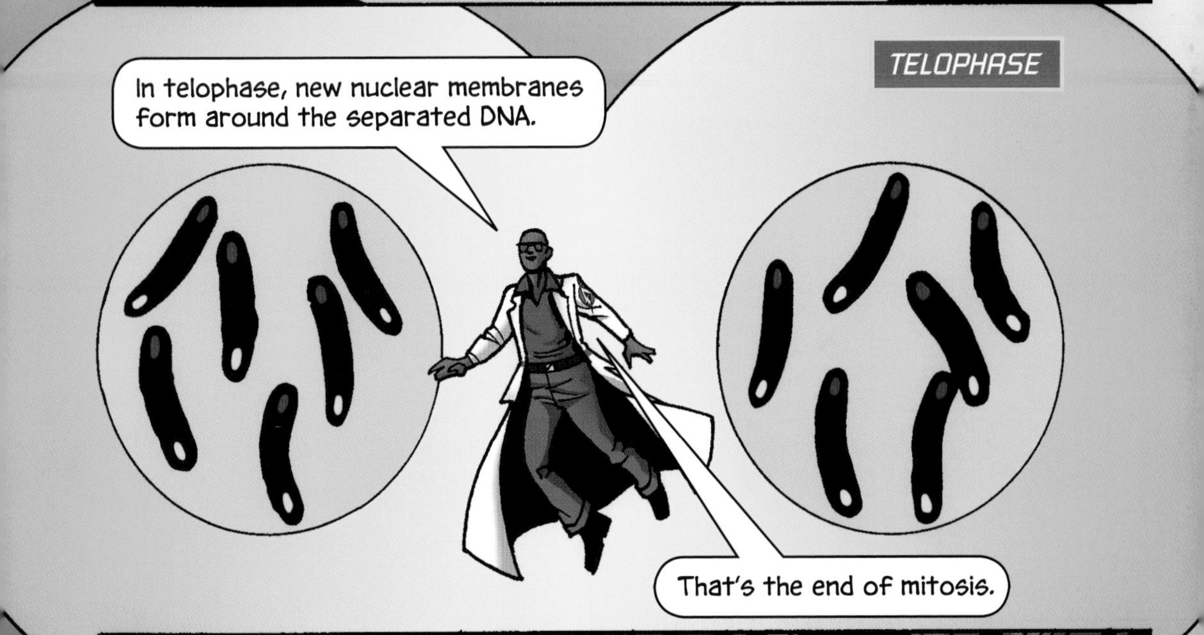
TELOPHASE
In telophase, new nuclear membranes form around the separated DNA.
That's the end of mitosis.

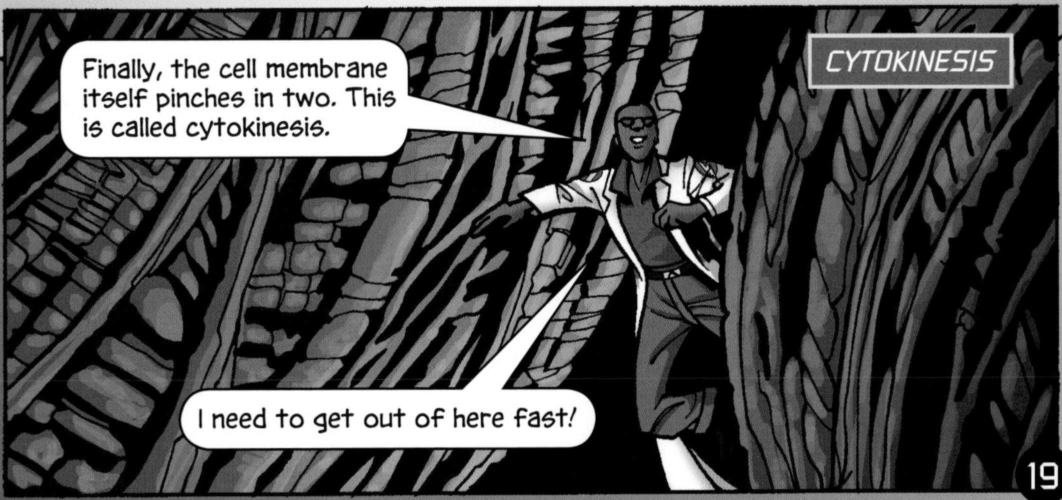
CYTOKINESIS
Finally, the cell membrane itself pinches in two. This is called cytokinesis.
I need to get out of here fast!

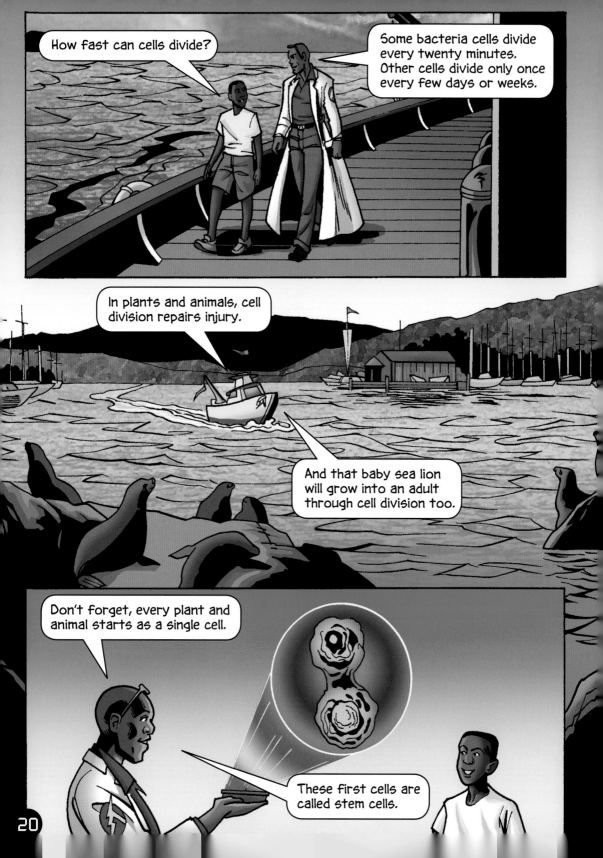

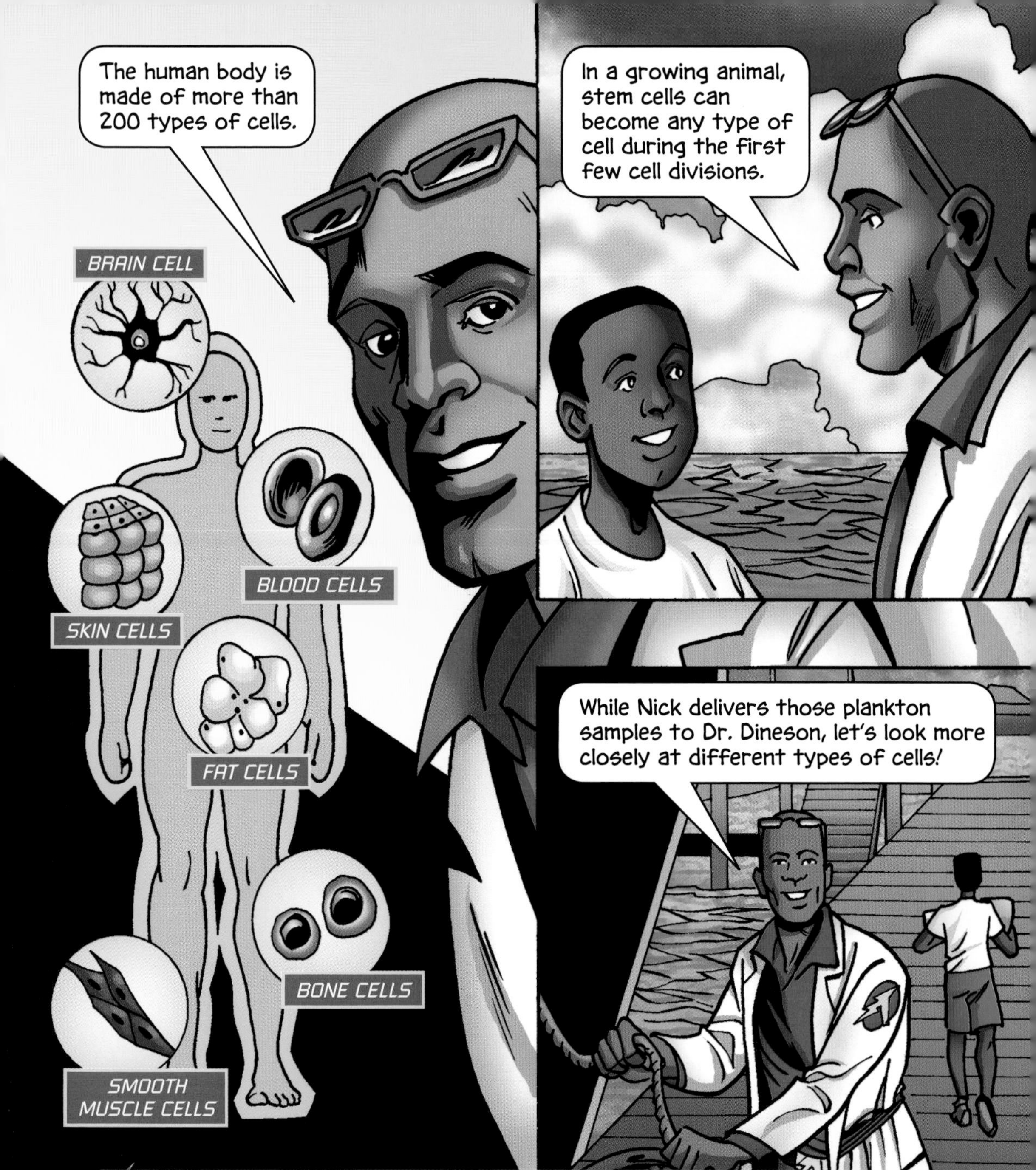
The human body is made of more than 200 types of cells.
BRAIN CELL
BLOOD CELLS
SKIN CELLS
FAT CELLS
BONE CELLS
SMOOTH MUSCLE CELLS
In a growing animal, stem cells can become any type of cell during the first few cell divisions.
While Nick delivers those plankton samples to Dr. Dineson, let's look more closely at different types of cells!

STEM CELLS IN MEDICINE

ACCESS GRANTED: MAX AXIOM

Scientists think that stem cells may be the answer to curing many diseases such as Parkinson's or Alzheimer's. Doctors may be able to use stem cells to replace old cells damaged by injury or disease. Bone marrow transplants are a form of stem cell therapy used to treat cancers like leukemia and lymphoma.

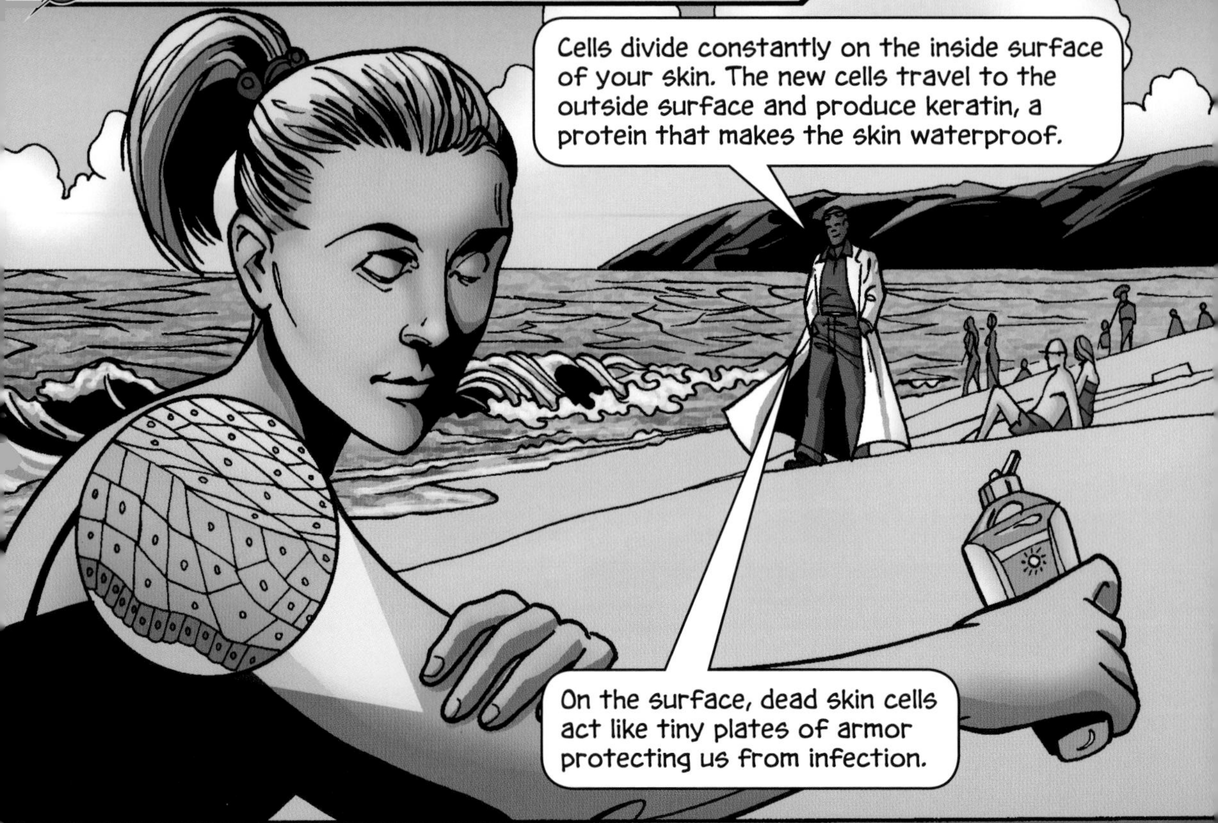
Cells divide constantly on the inside surface of your skin. The new cells travel to the outside surface and produce keratin, a protein that makes the skin waterproof.
On the surface, dead skin cells act like tiny plates of armor protecting us from infection.

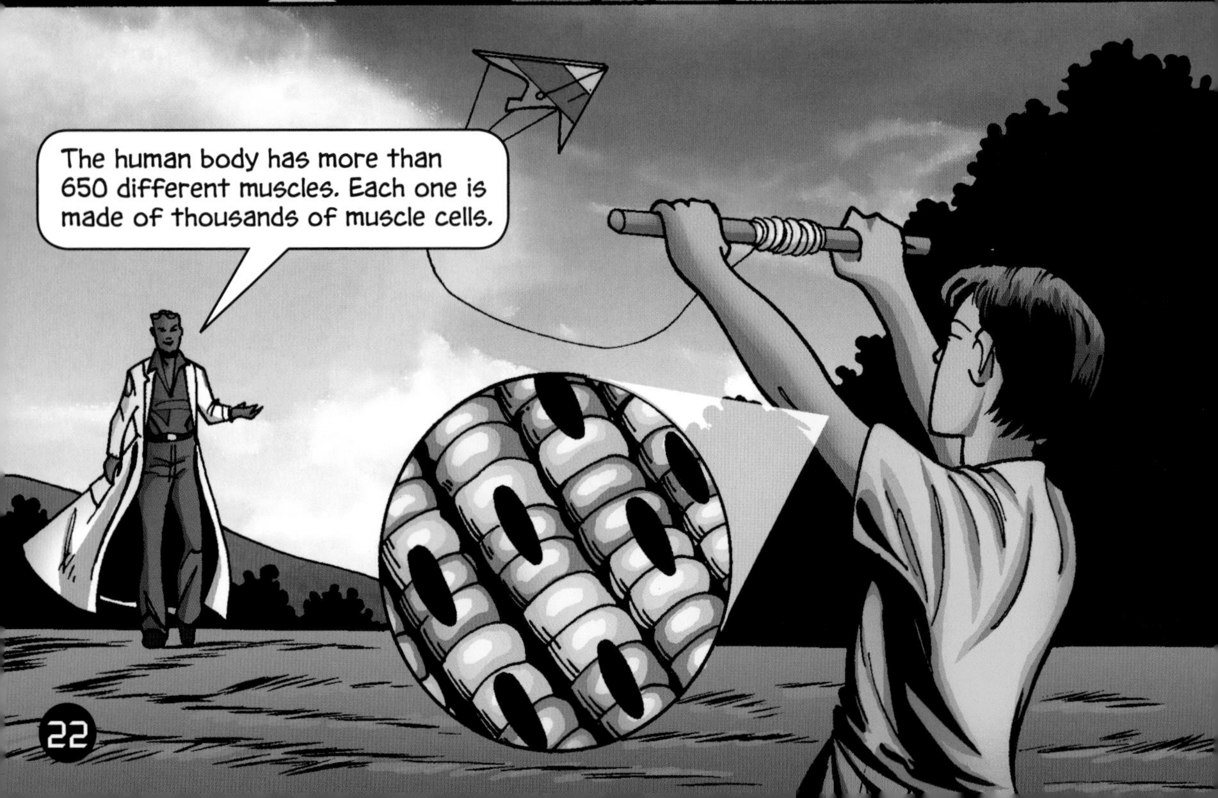
The human body has more than 650 different muscles. Each one is made of thousands of muscle cells.

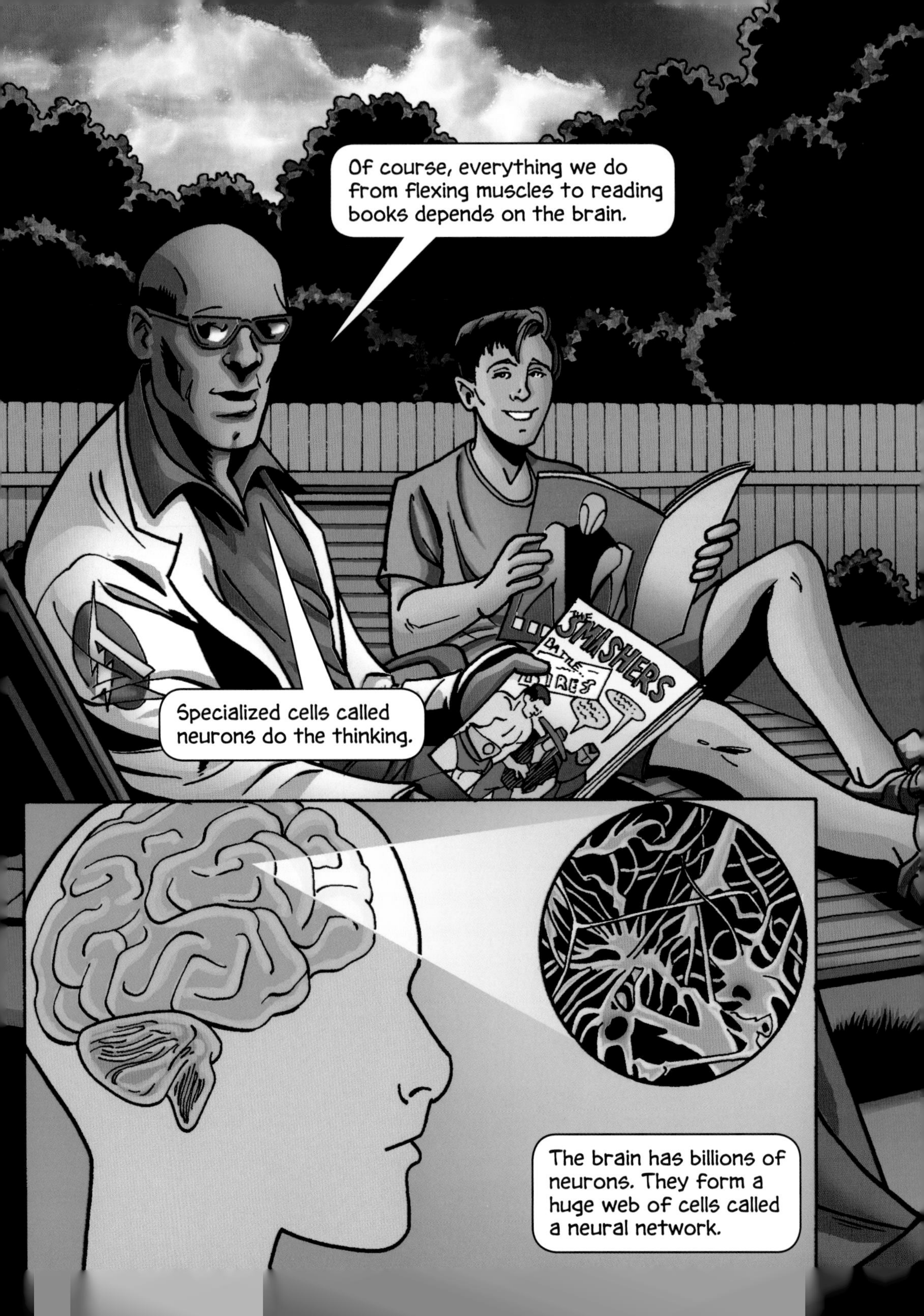
Of course, everything we do from flexing muscles to reading books depends on the brain.
Specialized cells called neurons do the thinking.
The brain has billions of neurons. They form a huge web of cells called a neural network.

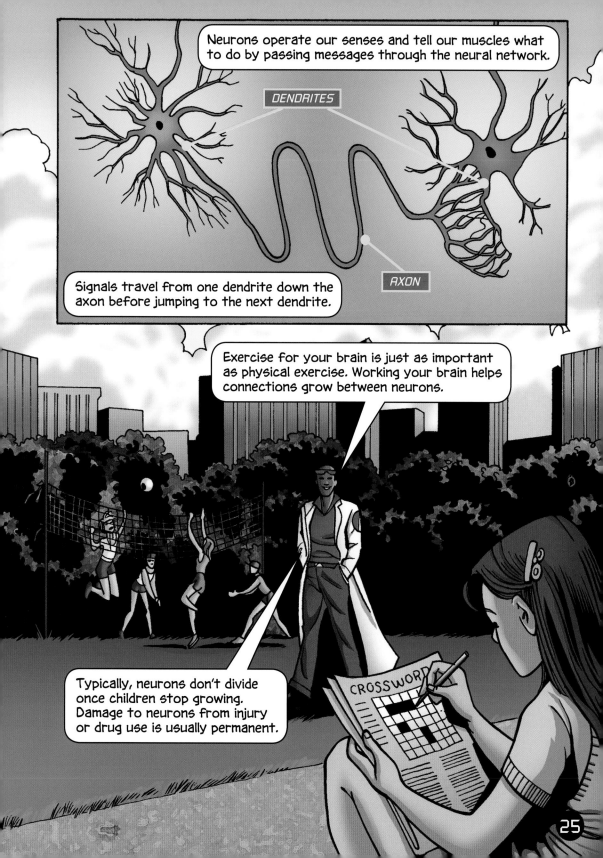

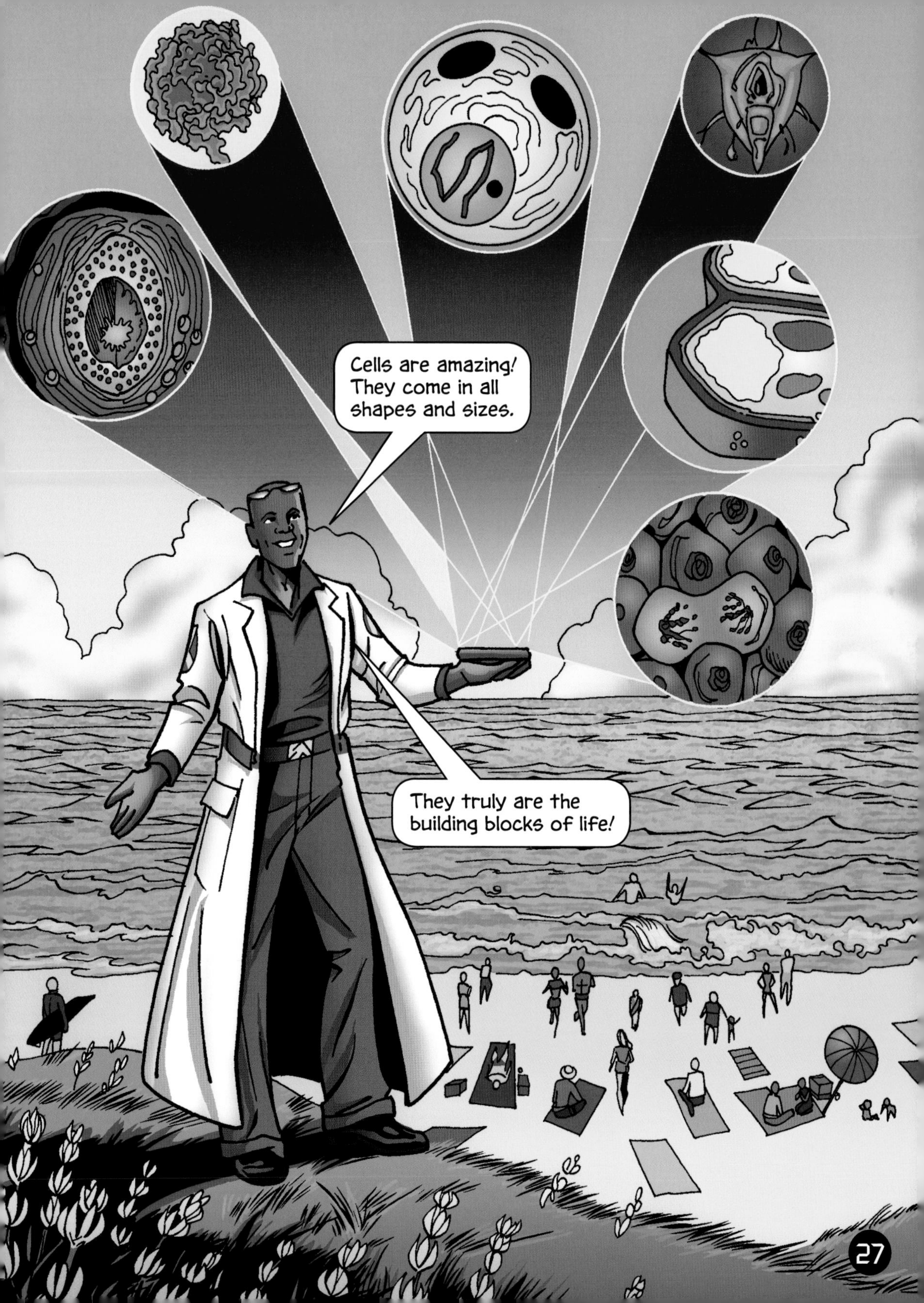
Cells are amazing! They come in all shapes and sizes.
They truly are the building blocks of life!

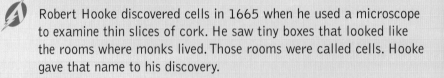

CELL LIFE

Robert Hooke discovered cells in 1665 when he used a microscope to examine thin slices of cork. He saw tiny boxes that looked like the rooms where monks lived. Those rooms were called cells. Hooke gave that name to his discovery.

In 1683, Anton van Leeuwenhoek built a microscope to observe bacteria found in his own mouth. He called them animalcules.

In 1839, scientists Matthias Schleiden and Theodor Schwann convinced the world that all living things are made of cells. An important part of cell theory is that all cells come from the division of other cells.

All cells are tiny, but they come in different shapes and sizes. The largest cells are found in frog eggs. They are nearly 0.04 inches (1 millimeter) in diameter. Fingerprint ridges are 20 cells wide. The neurons in the spinal cord can be 3 feet (0.9 meter) long.

Neurobiology, the study of the brain, is an exciting area of medical research. Scientists use Magnetic Resonance Imaging, or MRI, to take pictures of active neurons. These color photos show which parts of the brain are active when a person plays music or solves crossword puzzles.

Cell division is a complicated process. Damage to cells may cause them to divide and reproduce incorrectly. When this happens, cells grow in places they shouldn't. The resulting disease is called cancer.

One tool biologists use to study cells is called a cell culture. A cell culture is a sample of cells that is kept alive in the laboratory through continuous cell division. In 1951, cells were taken from a woman who had cancer. Her cells have been dividing ever since. Scientists use these cells in their research.

 Dehydration is more dangerous than starvation because the cytoplasm of cells is made mostly of water. Without water, nothing inside the cell will work correctly. Humans can survive without eating for much longer than they can go without water because cells can use energy stored in fat cells.

MORE ABOUT

SUPER SCIENTIST

Real name: **Maxwell J. Axiom**
Hometown: **Seattle, Washington**
Height: **6' 1"**   Weight: **192 lbs**
Eyes: **Brown**   Hair: **None**

Super capabilities: Super intelligence; able to shrink to the size of an atom; sunglasses give x-ray vision; lab coat allows for travel through time and space.

Origin: Since birth, Max Axiom seemed destined for greatness. His mother, a marine biologist, taught her son about the mysteries of the sea. His father, a nuclear physicist and volunteer park ranger, schooled Max on the wonders of earth and sky.

One day on a wilderness hike, a megacharged lightning bolt struck Max with blinding fury. When he awoke, Max discovered a newfound energy and set out to learn as much about science as possible. He traveled the globe earning degrees in every aspect of the field. Upon his return, he was ready to share his knowledge and new identity with the world. He had become Max Axiom, Super Scientist.

GLOSSARY

amino acid (uh-MEE-noh ASS-id) — a basic building block of protein that contains nitrogen; amino acids can be made by the body or ingested through eating foods with protein.

ATP (AY TEE PEE) — a molecule that provides energy to cells

cellulose (SEL-yuh-lohss) — the substance from which the cell walls of plants are made

DNA (DEE EN AY) — the genetic material that carries all of the instructions to make a living thing and keep it working; DNA stands for deoxyribonucleic acid.

gene (JEEN) — a part of every cell that carries physical and behavioral information passed from parents to their children

glucose (GLOO-kose) — a natural sugar found in plants that gives energy to living things

metabolism (muh-TAB-uh-liz-uhm) — the process of changing food into energy

mitosis (mye-TOE-sis) — the process of cell division where one nucleus divides into two creating two identical cells

organelle (or-guh-NELL) — a small structure in a cell that performs a specific function and is surrounded by its own membrane

photosynthesis (foh-toh-SIN-thuh-siss) — the process by which green plants make their food

plankton (PLANGK-tuhn) — microscopic plants and animals that live in water

stem cell (STEM SELL) — a cell from which other types of cells can develop

READ MORE

Freedman, Jeri. *America Debates Stem Cell Research.* America Debates. New York: Rosen Central, 2008.

Johnson, Rebecca L. *Ultra-Organized Cell Systems.* Microquests. Minneapolis: Millbrook Press, 2008.

Silverstein, Alvin. *Cells.* Science Concepts. Minneapolis: Twenty-First Century Books, 2009.

Snedden, Robert. *The World of the Cell: Life on a Small Scale.* Cells & Life. Chicago: Heinemann, 2008.

Spilsbury, Richard. *Cells, Tissues, and Organs.* The Human Machine. Chicago: Heinemann, 2008.

Stille, Darlene R. *Cells.* Gareth Stevens Vital Science. Pleasantville, N.Y.: Gareth Stevens, 2008.

INTERNET SITES

FactHound offers a safe, fun way to find Internet sites related to this book. All sites on FactHound have been researched by our staff.

Here's all you do:

Visit *www.facthound.com*

FactHound will fetch the best sites for you!

INDEX